1992

S0-BHW-060

NOV 12 1996

3 9082 02606016 3

COPY 19

J
782.1   Botsford, Ward.
B   The pirates of Penzance / adapted
          from the Gilbert & Sullivan operetta by
          Ward Botsford ; illustrated by Edward
          Sorel. New York : Random House, 1981.

             unpaged : ill.   bfc 5-9

             SUMMARY: Retells in prose the story
          about a group of pirates who can't seem
          to make piracy pay and who fall in love
          with the ten daughters of a major gen-
          eral.

             ISBN 0-394-94993-5 (lib. bdg.) : 9.99

             1. Operas--Stories, plots, etc.   65190

                                          81-5173   YA D82
                                          CIP MAEC MN

Allen Road

The Pirates of Penzance

The Story of the Gilbert & Sullivan Operetta

Adapted by WARD BOTSFORD
Illustrated by EDWARD SOREL

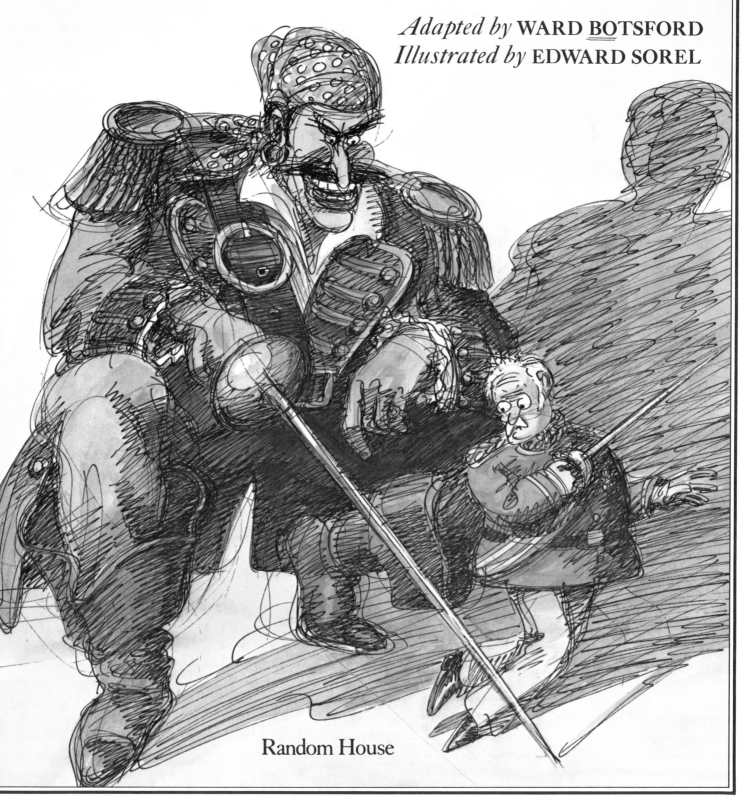

Random House

To Lynn because . . .
W. B.

AN EXPLANATORY NOTE

William S. Gilbert wrote *The Pirates of Penzance* in 1879, and by now some of the words and phrases he used in the lyrics have fallen out of use. For this reason, a few brief notes have been included at the end of this book that explain the more difficult or outdated Victorian terms in the songs.

Text Copyright © 1981 by Ward Botsford. Illustrations Copyright © 1981 by Edward Sorel. All rights reserved under International and Pan-American Copyright Conventions. Published in the United States by Random House, Inc., New York, and simultaneously in Canada by Random House of Canada Limited, Toronto.
Library of Congress Cataloging in Publication Data: Botsford, Ward. The pirates of Penzance. SUMMARY: Retells in prose the story about a group of pirates who can't seem to make piracy pay and who fall in love with the ten daughters of a major-general.   1. Sullivan, Arthur, Sir, 1842–1900. Pirates of Penzance.   2. Sullivan, Arthur, Sir, 1842–1900—Stories of operas—Juvenile.   [1. Operas—Stories, plots, etc.]   I. Gilbert, W.S. (William Schwenck), 1836–1911. Pirates of Penzance.   II. Sullivan, Arthur, Sir, 1842–1900. Pirates of Penzance. III. Sorel, Edward, 1929– . IV. Title.   ML3930.S95B73   782.1'3   81-5173   AACR2   ISBN: 0-394-84993-0 (trade); 0-394-94993-5 (lib. bdg.) Manufactured in the United States of America   1 2 3 4 5 6 7 8 9 0

J
782.1
Bo

On the southern coast of England, jutting out into the Atlantic, there is a lovely little seaport called Penzance. Near Penzance are great cliffs and a line of rocks sticking out into the sea. It looks to be just the place for pirates. And indeed, it once was.

There, a little more than a hundred years ago, lying at anchor off the shore, was a great schooner. It flew the skull and crossbones of the *Jolly Roger*. On the beach the pirates from the schooner were celebrating, singing loudly and drinking. In those days ordinary pirates drank rum, but these pirates were filling their glasses with fine sherry, for they were English pirates and civilized men one and all!

"Gentlemen pirates," called the Pirate Lieutenant, raising his glass, "let us drink to Frederick, who today turns twenty-one and ends his pirate apprenticeship. To Frederick— welcome to our ranks as a full-fledged pirate!"

Pour, oh pour the pirate sherry;
Fill, oh fill the pirate glass;
And, to make us more than merry,
Let the pirate bumper pass.

For today our pirate 'prentice
Rises from indenture freed;
Strong his arm and keen his scent is,
He's a pirate now indeed!

Here's good luck to Frederick's ventures!
Frederick's out of his indentures.

Frederick listened to the pirates' song with a sad smile on his face. "Gentlemen all, I thank you from the very bottom of my heart," he said. "But I now bid you all farewell, for I must leave your company."

"Leave us? Why?" The pirates gasped.

The Pirate King, his tricornered hat sitting rakishly on his periwig and his pistols thrust in his belt, swaggered up to Frederick. "Why, there is no better lad than you when it comes to cutting out a ship or scuttling a vessel," said the Pirate King. "And now, the very day you become a full member of our band, you say that you must leave us! My dear boy, tell me it is not true."

Frederick shook his head. "No, my mind is quite made up," he said. "I became an apprentice to you due to an unhappy error. I stayed with you because I am a slave of duty. The error was mine, not yours, but now I am twenty-one and free."

The pirates looked puzzled. "Error? What error?" asked the Pirate Lieutenant.

Frederick looked miserable. He did not want to answer them, for the truth would reflect poorly on Ruth, the pirates' maid-of-all-work and the only woman in their band. Frederick had known Ruth all his life. He thought her both charming and beautiful (she herself had told him that she was—again and again). Now Frederick glanced helplessly at her.

The plump, middle-aged Ruth smiled understandingly at Frederick. She sighed and patted his arm. "Come, Frederick," she said. "It's better to have it out so all may know the truth." And she told the pirates how Frederick had, through her error, joined them:

> When Frederick was a little lad he proved so
>   brave and daring,
> His father thought he'd 'prentice him to some
>   career seafaring.
> I was, alas! his nurserymaid, and so it fell to my
>   lot
> To take and bind the promising boy apprentice
>   to a pilot.
> A life not bad for a hardy lad, though surely not
>   a high lot.
> Though I'm a nurse, you might do worse, than
>   make your boy a pilot.
> I was a stupid nurserymaid, on breakers always
>   steering,
> And I did not catch the word aright, through
>   being hard of hearing.
> Mistaking my instructions, which within my
>   brain did gyrate,
> I took and bound this promising boy apprentice
>   to a pirate.
> A sad mistake it was to make and doom him to a
>   vile lot.
> I bound him to a pirate—you—instead of to a
>   pilot.

At this Ruth broke into tears, and Frederick tried to comfort her. He assured her that he had long ago forgiven her the error that made him a pirate instead of a pilot. But Ruth just sobbed harder and harder. By then the pirates were all in tears themselves, so touched were they by Ruth's heartfelt confession.

"I must now depart," sighed Frederick, "for while I love you one and all, still you must admit that being a pirate is not one of the most honest professions." Here Frederick began weeping too. "And to make amends for my previous years spent as a pirate, I must now devote myself to your complete extermination!" Then Frederick repeated hastily, "Although I love you one and all."

"Well, Frederick," said the Pirate King as he wiped his eyes, "if you must exterminate us, then you must! A man must always be guided by his conscience."

"Besides," put in the Pirate Lieutenant, "we can offer you but little to remain with us. We can't seem to make piracy pay. I don't know why, but we can't."

"*I* know why," said Frederick. "But I mustn't tell you now that you are about to become my enemy."

"My boy, you owe it to us to say why," said the Pirate King.

But Frederick just shook his head and folded his arms.

"Now, none of this," said the Pirate King reprovingly. "There are still twenty minutes before your contract expires. Until then you are still apprenticed to us, and I order that you give us an explanation—no more than twenty minutes long."

Because he was a slave to duty, Frederick

had to agree. "I will tell you," he said, "but only for twenty minutes."

All the pirates crowded around him.

"Your trouble is that you are too tenderhearted," said Frederick. "Good pirates always attack weaker ships, but not you! You always attack stronger ones. That is quite probably why you always lose. Then, too, you never molest orphans, rich or poor."

"Of course not!" protested the pirates. "We are all orphans ourselves."

"Yes, and by now everybody knows it," said Frederick. "So when you do manage to capture a few people, the first thing they tell you is that they are orphans. And you believe them, so instead of holding them for ransom, you release them!" Frederick felt sorry for his bungling pirate friends. "Ah, if only you would but give up being pirates and return with me to civilization and an honest life."

"Thank you, no," roared the Pirate King jovially. "Compared with civilization, our work is practically honest."

Oh, better far to live and die
Under the brave black flag I fly,
Than play a sanctimonious part,
With a pirate head and a pirate heart.
Away to the cheating world go you,
Where pirates all are well-to-do;
But I'll be true to the song I sing,
And live and die a Pirate King.
  For I am a Pirate King.

When I sally forth to seek my prey,
I help myself in a royal way:
I sink a few more ships, it's true,
Than a well-bred monarch ought to do;
But many a king on a first-class throne,
If he wants to call his crown his own,
Must manage somehow to get through
More dirty work than ever I do,
  For I am a Pirate King.

The pirates joined in their leader's song. Then they climbed into their dinghy and began rowing out to the schooner. Ruth stayed on the beach, imploring Frederick to take her with him.

"But Ruth," said Frederick, "I am a lad of twenty-one, and you are a girl of forty-seven. I have not seen another woman since I was a boy of eight. Tell me, how do you compare with other women? Be honest now—are you *really* beautiful?"

"I have been told so . . . many years ago,"

said Ruth coyly. "And I am still a beauty," she added fervently.

Frederick smiled fondly at her. "Yes, I believe you, for I am certain that a girl of forty-seven would not lie about her beauty."

Just then they heard a chorus of giggling voices coming from behind some nearby rocks. "Who can that possibly be?" asked Frederick.

"Ruination! The voices of young maidens," said Ruth to herself. "If he sees them, I am lost!"

Frederick climbed the rocks to get a

better view. What met his eyes left him breathless with surprise and delight!

"Why, it's a bevy of beautiful maidens!" he gasped. "And the plainest is more beautiful than Ruth." He called down to Ruth, "You have deceived me!" And Frederick's forty-seven-year-old maid-of-all-work fled in despair.

Frederick did not want the lovely girls to see him in his pirate garb. He quickly ran to a nearby cave. No sooner had he hidden himself than ten young girls appeared over the rocks.

"Oh! How enchanting!" they babbled.

"Yes," said one. "Why, fancy! Perhaps we are the first people ever to set foot in this lovely place."

Then another suggested that while waiting for their father to catch up with them, they might take off their shoes and stockings and paddle about in the sea. All ten girls immediately took off their left shoes.

It was then that a red-faced Frederick came out of his hiding place. "Stop, ladies, pray!" he called out.

"A man!" shrieked the maidens all together as they hopped about the beach.

Frederick apologized for his intrusion. "I had intended to remain hidden, but when I overheard your intention to disrobe, I could not, as a gentleman, remain silent."

"May we ask who you are, sir?" asked one of the girls.

Frederick hung his head and in a voice that could hardly be heard said, "I am a pirate."

All ten girls sprang back in terror. "A pirate? Horrors!"

"Please, fair ladies!" implored Frederick. "This very day I left my vile profession. Is

there not one among you who can look with pity on me? If you will cast a kindly eye on me, however plain you are—I will love you!"

All of the maidens were silent.

"Not even one?" asked Frederick sadly.

Then one of the maidens stepped forward. "Yes, one!" she said.

"Mabel!" squealed the other nine.

"Yes, my sisters, if this lad has gone astray, then it is our duty to help him," said Mabel. And turning to Frederick she sang:

Poor wandering one!
Though thou hast surely strayed.
    Take heart of grace,
    Thy steps retrace,
Poor wandering one!
Poor wandering one!
If such poor love as mine
    Can help thee find
    True peace of mind—
Why take it, it is thine!
Take heart, fair days will shine;
Take any heart—take mine!

Frederick saw at once that Mabel was quite the loveliest of the ten sisters. He listened to her song with a moonstruck look upon his face, and when she finished he moved to her. They clasped hands and began talking intently to each other.

Mabel's sisters were shocked. But being well-brought-up ladies, they launched into a lively discussion of the weather (all the while trying to eavesdrop on their sister and Frederick).

Suddenly Frederick remembered the pirates. He advised the sisters to leave at once before the pirates spotted them.

But it was too late to escape, for the

pirates had returned and had been listening from behind the rocks. They bounded into the midst of the frightened sisters with cries of "Ha! Ha! Ha!"

Here's a first-rate opportunity
To get married with impunity;
And indulge in the felicity
Of unbounded domesticity.

The pirates meant to marry the girls one and all!

But Mabel—the brave Mabel—spoke out. "Monsters!" she exclaimed. "You cannot marry us against our will! Our father is a Major-General!"

This gave the pirates pause, and before they could respond, a voice behind them said, "Yes, I am a Major-General."

There, dressed in full regalia, with medals gleaming on his breast and a plume in his hat, was Major-General Stanley of the British army. He stood with his chin held high and his hand upon the hilt of his sword. Then he very carefully explained to the pirates the importance of being a Major-General.

> I am the very model of a modern Major-General,
> I've information vegetable, animal, and mineral;
> I know the kings of England, and I quote the fights historical,
> From Marathon to Waterloo, in order categorical;
> I'm very well acquainted too with matters mathematical,
> I understand equations, both the simple and quadratical,
> About binomial theorem I'm teeming with a lot o' news—
> With many cheerful facts about the square of the hypotenuse.
> I know our mythic history, King Arthur's and Sir Caradoc's,
> I answer hard acrostics, I've a pretty taste for paradox.
> I quote in elegiacs all the crimes of Heliogabalus,
> In conics I can floor peculiarities parabolus.
> I can tell undoubted Raphaels from Gerard Dows and Zoffanies,
> I know the croaking chorus from the "Frogs" of Aristophanes.
> Then I can hum a fugue of which I've heard the music's din afore,
> And whistle all the airs from that infernal nonsense "Pinafore."
> Then I can write a washing bill in Babylonic cuneiform,
> And tell you every detail of Caractacus's uniform;
> In short, in matters vegetable, animal, and mineral,
> I am the very model of a modern Major-General.
>
> In fact, when I know what is meant by "mamelon" and "ravelin,"
> When I can tell at sight a mauser rifle from a javelin,
> When such affairs as sorties and surprises I'm more wary at,
> And when I know precisely what is meant by commissariat,
> When I have learnt what progress has been made in modern gunnery,
> When I know more of tactics than a novice in a nunnery;
> In short, when I've a smattering of elemental strategy,
> You'll say a better Major-General has never sat a gee—
> For my military knowledge, though I'm plucky and adventury,
> Has only been brought down to the beginning of the century;
> But still in matters vegetable, animal, and mineral,
> I am the very model of a modern Major-General.

"And now," said Major-General Stanley, clicking his heels, "since I have introduced myself, pray tell me what is going on."

The Pirate Lieutenant strode up to the Major-General. "Let me explain," he said, bowing low. "We are going to marry your daughters."

"Against our will!" cried the girls.

"May I ask," said the Major-General, "who you are in these . . . ahh . . . picturesque uniforms?"

The Pirate King swept off his hat. "We are single gentlemen and—"

"Papa," interrupted Mabel, "they are the infamous pirates of Penzance."

"Ah, yes, I've heard of you, of course," said the Major-General. "But as it happens, I don't want pirates as sons-in-law."

The pirates laughed.

"Well," responded the Pirate King, "as it happens, we don't want a Major-General for a father-in-law either. But we'll overlook it."

How could he get these ruffians to abandon their plan to marry his daughters? That was the knotty problem that faced the Major-General. Then he remembered something he had heard about the pirates of Penzance.

"Very well," said the Major-General, "but if you marry my daughters one and all, I

will be left quite alone. Tell me," he continued with the deepest of sighs, "do you know what it is like to be left alone . . . *when you are an orphan?*"

"Oh, bother," exclaimed the pirates. "It's happened again! Another orphan! What bad luck. We can't deprive an orphan of his only family." And, being soft-hearted, they gave up their plan to marry the Major-General's daughters.

"Thieves we may be," said the Pirate King, "and pirates too. And we may sink a ship or two. But we are not devoid of feeling, so we will let you go."

Frederick then asked the Major-General for permission to marry Mabel. Since the Major-General had no objections to a *reformed* pirate as a son-in-law, he quickly gave his consent. Frederick and Mabel were ecstatically happy.

The pirates unfurled the skull and cross-bones and marched off in one direction. Major-General Stanley unfurled the British flag and, with the girls and Frederick, marched off in the opposite direction.

Once back at his ancestral home (which he had bought the year before), Major-General Stanley fell into a state of depression. He had lied to the pirates. True, his story about being an orphan had saved his daughters from a fate worse than death. But lying was a terrible thing for a Major-General to do.

Frederick and Mabel tried to cheer him. They told him that that very night Frederick would most certainly sweep the pirates from the face of the earth.

The Major-General perked up. "And have you followers at hand to help, my boy?"

"Indeed, I do. They but await my orders, sir," said Frederick, and he turned and called, "Enter!"

In they came, in single file, a line of policemen, looking more than a little unhappy.

When the foeman bears his steel,
    Tarantara! tarantara!
We uncomfortable feel,
    Tarantara!
And we find the wisest thing,
    Tarantara! tarantara!
Is to slap our chests and sing
    Tarantara!
For when threatened with emeutes,
    Tarantara! tarantara!
And your heart is in your boots,
    Tarantara!
There is nothing brings it round,
Like the trumpet's martial sound,
    Tarantara! tarantara!

And Mabel made them even more nervous by singing "Go, ye heroes, go to glory! Though you die in combat gory."

The police thanked Mabel but added that, while her intentions were probably well-meant . . .

Such expressions don't appear,
    Tarantara! tarantara!
Calculated men to cheer,
    Tarantara! tarantara!
Who are going to meet their fate
In a highly nervous state,
    Tarantara!

"Well, then," said Major-General Stanley, "off you go to meet your fate."

"Yes, off we go . . ." they said, but made no move.

"Yes, well, go then. Go!" commanded the Major-General.

The policemen marched off reluctantly with Mabel bringing up the rear and urging them on. Frederick was about to join them when, suddenly, in burst the Pirate King and Ruth. Both were armed with pistols, which they pointed at Frederick.

"Hear me!" said Frederick to the Pirate King. "I have resolved on your slaughter. Nothing you say or do will stop me!"

"Well," said the Pirate King, twirling his pistol, "before the slaughter commences—and I hope, dear Frederick, that you will be merciful—we have an amusing story to tell you. We know how you have always enjoyed a paradox or two."

"And you've come all the way here, risking capture, to tell me an amusing story?" asked Frederick, scarcely believing his ears. "Well, what is it?"

The Pirate King stroked his chin and began. "The month of February has but twenty-eight days, and then every four years one additional day is added to make it twenty-nine days. Leap year, you know."

Frederick nodded, hardly knowing what was coming next.

"Well, Frederick, my brave lad, you were born on February the twenty-ninth. Consequently, if you'll do a bit of mathematics, you'll find that while you've lived twenty-one years, still, as birthdays go, you've only had five birthdays. So you're only five, and a little bit."

Greatly amazed, Frederick figured it out with pencil and paper. "Why, yes, I do believe you're right. Only five! Surely I don't look it!"

"But," added the Pirate King, "isn't it lucky we discovered it in time? Wouldn't it have been terrible if you'd killed your comrades not having known? Your apprenticeship was to last until your twenty-first birthday, and you are only five and a little bit. You see, it says twenty-one *birthdays* in the paper your father signed—not twenty-one *years*. A paradox, a most ingenious paradox! Ha! ha! ha! ha! Ho! ho! ho! ho!"

"It does rather change things," said Frederick with a bowed head. "As I am a slave to duty, I suppose I must rejoin your pirate crew until my twenty-first birthday."

The Pirate King and Ruth nodded.

"In that case, it is my duty as a pirate apprentice to confess that the Major-General was not entirely truthful. He is not now, nor has he ever been, an orphan," said Frederick sadly.

"What! Not an orphan?" exclaimed the Pirate King, greatly shocked. "He has lied to us! He has cheated us of our brides! Our revenge, dear Frederick, will be sudden and terrible! This very night we shall capture the Major-General and his daughters! And you, my boy, must join us! I'll expect you shortly."

No sooner had the Pirate King and Ruth left than Mabel returned. "On to victory! Your gallant crew of policemen await your command!" she said. Then she noticed Frederick's heartsick expression. "My dear Frederick, what ails you?" she asked.

Frederick told Mabel of his leap-year birthday and its unhappy consequences for him. "I will not have my twenty-first birthday until—until—why, not until the distant year of 1940," he said, "at which time I will be eighty-two years old! Mabel, will you wait for me?"

Without a second's hesitation Mabel replied, "Of course, Frederick, I would wait for you forever."

"Then, my dearest Mabel, I must say adieu!" And with that Frederick departed to rejoin the pirates.

Meanwhile, the policemen, though still unhappy about it, had resigned themselves to doing battle. Ready now for Frederick to lead

them to the pirates, they returned to the Major-General's ancestral home. Mabel greeted them tearfully and explained why Frederick had left. Then she told the police that they would have to fight the pirates on their own.

"We will do our best by ourselves," said the police sergeant, "but it seems unfair that we must chase our fellow creatures."

When a felon's not engaged in his employment—
     His employment,
Or maturing his felonious little plans—
     Little plans,
His capacity for innocent enjoyment—
     'Cent enjoyment,
Is just as great as any honest man's—
     Honest man's.
Our feelings we with difficulty smother—
     'Culty smother,
When constabulary duty's to be done—
     To be done.

Ah, take one consideration with another—
     With another,
A policeman's lot is not a happy one.
When the enterprising burglar's not a-burgling—
     Not a-burgling,
When the cut-throat isn't occupied in crime—
     'Pied in crime,
He loves to hear the little brook a-gurgling—
     Brook a-gurgling,
And listen to the merry village chime—
     Village chime.
When constabulary duty's to be done—
     To be done,
The policeman's lot is not a happy one—
     Happy one.

Then, off in the distance, the police heard the rousing battle cry of the pirates! They began shaking like leaves. Led by their brave sergeant, they quickly hid themselves.

The pirates, including an unhappy Frederick and a doleful Ruth, crept toward the castle cautiously, for they wished to take the Major-General by surprise. They came fully prepared, not only with the weapons of their trade—swords and pistols—but with a remarkable assortment of burglars' tools should a forced entry be necessary.

> With catlike tread,
>> Upon our prey we steal,
> In silence dread
>> Our cautious way we feel.
> No sound at all,
>> We never speak a word,
> A fly's foot-fall
>> Would be distinctly heard.

The pirates were terrible burglars. Despite what they said, they clanked and stumbled about very noisily.

"Hush, I see a light!" whispered Frederick. "The Major-General comes. Let us hide!"

His shameful lie about being an orphan had been weighing heavily on the honorable Major-General's conscience. Unable to sleep, he had been wandering through the halls of his castle when he thought he heard a noise. His daughters also thought they heard a noise. Lighting their way with candles, they came downstairs to investigate and found their father.

Seeing the girls and their father, the Pirate King attacked! Springing from their hiding places, the pirates quickly surrounded the surprised Major-General and his family.

"Frederick, save us!" cried Mabel.

"Beautiful Mabel, I would if I could but I am not able," replied Frederick sadly.

It was now or never for the timid police! Led by their quaking sergeant, the police jumped from their hiding places and confronted the pirates directly. Although the pirates were not terribly good at doing battle, at least they had weapons. As you may know, English policemen *never* carry weapons. So, in no time at all, the police were forced to the floor by the pirates, who stood over them in a rare moment of victory.

"Your proud triumph will quickly fade, for we have a surprise for you," said the sergeant.

"Oh no," said the Pirate King. "Don't say you are orphans, for we know that game."

"No," said the sergeant, drawing himself up and thrusting out his chest. "We call upon you to yield, in Queen Victoria's name!"

Loyal subjects to the core, the pirates fell to their knees the instant they heard the name of their Queen.

"We yield at once," said the Pirate King humbly, "for with all our faults, we love our Queen."

The police made haste to seize the pirates, but they did so weeping openly—so touched were they by the pirates' loyalty to the Queen.

The Major-General smoothed his dressing gown and ordered the sergeant to take the pirates before the bar of justice. But Ruth, the piratical maid-of-all-work, suddenly spoke up:

> One moment! Let me tell you who they are.
> They are no members of the common throng;
> They are all noblemen, who have gone wrong!

The policemen were amazed, and the Major-General was also greatly impressed. "What!" he exclaimed. "Noblemen from our

House of Peers! Why, then they are all gentlemen!" Suddenly the Major-General saw the pirates in a more favorable light. "We must forgive those who have gone astray, especially noblemen, for we English dearly love our House of Peers, whatever their faults."

I pray you pardon me, ex-Pirate King,
Peers will be peers, and youth will have its fling.
Resume your ranks, and legislative duties,
And take my daughters, all of whom are beauties.

The ex-Pirate King bowed and promptly accepted the Major-General's offer. Mabel and Frederick embraced joyfully. And Major-General Stanley, pleased that he had so tidily married off his daughters, said:

My military knowledge, though I'm plucky and adventury,
Has only been brought down to the beginning of the century;
But still, in getting off my daughters—eight or nine or ten in all—
I've shown myself the model of a modern Major-General.

EXPLANATORY NOTES

OPENING CHORUS. Each of the pirates toasts Frederick with a *bumper,* or full glass, of sherry. They are celebrating the end of his *indenture,* or apprenticeship, to the Pirate King.

THE PIRATE KING'S SONG. Here the Pirate King expresses his dislike of *sanctimonious,* "respectable" people, who only pretend to be good. He would much rather live his life of piracy and crime openly, and *sally forth,* or go forth, without pretense.

THE PIRATES' SONG. The Pirates sing in praise of marriage. *Impunity* means without risk or harm; *felicity* means happiness; and *domesticity* means having to do with the home.

THE MAJOR-GENERAL'S SONG. Major-General Stanley tries to impress everyone with his superior military knowledge by reeling off a bewildering series of names, places, and things. He starts off with *Marathon,* a battle fought in Greece in 490 B.C., and *Waterloo,* a battle fought in Belgium in 1815. Then, in order *categorical,* or as the words occur, he gives us a list of terms used in mathematics: *quadratical, binomial theorem,* and *hypotenuse.* Next he mentions *Sir Caradoc,* a knight living at the time of King Arthur, and *Heliogabalus,* a Roman emperor. *Acrostics* are word puzzles, and *elegiacs* are a kind of poem, often expressing sorrow. A *paradox* is something that seems to contradict itself, is puzzling, or is very hard to believe—like Frederick's situation. *Conic* and *parabolus* are two geometrical terms. *Raphaels, Gerard Dows,* and *Zoffanies* are paintings done by Raphael, an Italian painter, Gerard Dow, a Dutch painter, and Zoffany, a German painter. The great Greek playwright *Aristophanes* did write *"The Frogs,"* though there is no croaking chorus in it, and *that infernal nonsense "Pinafore"* is a wonderfully funny operetta that Gilbert wrote in 1878. *Babylonic cuneiform* is a very ancient kind of writing, and *Caractacus* was a British king in the first century. Next the Major-General moves on to things military: a *mamelon* is a small hill, *ravelin* means part of the outside of a fort, a *mauser* is a German rifle, and a *javelin* is a spear. When the Major-General says *"sat a gee,"* he's talking about riding a horse.

THE POLICEMEN'S SONG. A *foeman* is a criminal, his *steel* is his knife, and *emeutes* is an old French word meaning disturbance, or riot.

THE POLICE SERGEANT'S SONG. A *felon* is a criminal, and the *constabulary* are the police.